G000069640

PAPER WORDS

A compilation of short writings,
to encourage, comfort and support.

Neti

DEDICATION

To the One that is Love,
and is that which sustains
us all.
And to you the reader,
who is a part of that Love.

CONTENTS

INTRODUCTION

We are both ordinary and extraordinary people, living both ordinary and extraordinary lives. Hopefully, we all have plenty of joy and happiness in our lives. We do also, all have a certain amount of suffering as well, that is for sure. Not one of us will escape it! The best that we can do, is to learn how to live every aspect of our lives well. To manage that, would be quite some achievement! When it comes to the joy and happiness, well, generally speaking, it tends to take care of itself. The suffering, is not quite so straight forward. Learning how to live our suffering well, and how to transform it into healing, takes courage, determination, and the faith to believe that it will happen. We all need to have good Teachers, who have trodden the path for themselves, and who know what it is like to suffer. Teachers who are willing to walk with us for a while, when we are suffering, so that we might lean on them and learn their ways. The writings in this book, are an offering to you. They are an offer of support to you, whilst you transform your own suffering, and learn to love yourself well. Hopefully, they will help you to realise your own personal Truth, about just how

extraordinarily wonderful you are, and of course, how loved.

The writings contain a lot of references to the 'One', and 'Me', and one may well ask "Who, or what are they?" Part of our journey, is about finding the answer to that question for ourselves.

The book contains fifty small writings, each one no more than a page long. The aim of each one, is to inspire, comfort, and heal the reader, at all levels of their being (physically, emotionally, psychologically, and spiritually). The writings are a reminder to the reader, of their true worth, beauty, and magnificence. They are also a reminder of the One love that underlies all things.

FORWARD

Our own life journey, is the most important journey we will ever undertake. It is the biggest challenge, and the greatest adventure. We are born into the 'mud of the earth', and our journey is about finding our way back to 'heaven'. Mostly, we travel 'blind', and often do not know how to travel well, or which path to take. I have been so fortunate, as to have had so many Teachers, guide me on my way. The writings in this book, are the unspoken 'songs', that those people have, by the example of their love, in some way, taught me to sing; the silent songs, that have arisen in my own heart, as I have learned to recognise the Truth of love, that is singing in theirs. I feel inexpressible gratitude to them all!

To My child, wherever you are.

There are some things I have been wanting to say to you:

When you were born, it was as if a beautiful little 'sparkle of Light' had come into My life. My heart leapt within My chest I felt such joy. You were so perfectly perfect in every way. I laughed with delight, and My love for you was instant and total.

Throughout your life, you have blessed Me beyond measure, and I have celebrated you in everything you have done. I have shared your hopes and dreams, and longed for your happiness to be complete.

My dearest, most beloved child, take My blessing now and live in joy; live fully and completely, knowing that you were born into love, and are everything I could have wished for.

You are beautiful.
You are lovely.
You are Divine Love.
You are bliss.
You are joy.
You are happiness.
You are a 'diamond' in the universe.
You are a 'jewel beyond price'.
Arise and shine.
Arise and have life.
Arise and live your dreams.
Arise and smile at the world.
You are the love that you yourself needs.
Embrace yourself and be alive.

Please do not think, that you have to keep
your pain and suffering to yourself.
Please do not think, that you are all alone,
and that you must hide your fear and
trembling.
When you dare to show Me your suffering,
you give Me permission to love you.
I have suffering of My own, and I need your
love too.
We can walk together, you and Me. We can
walk hand in hand.

My dear child,
Whatever the feeling, however intense,
surrender it to the Divine.
The suffering you have experienced at the
hands of others, was just them trying to
survive, without knowing a better way.
Your life will be powerful, full, and free.
Feel the shame, the anger, the hurt, but
also remember, the astonishing light of
your own True Self.

Dear child,

You have not done anything wrong. You are wholly innocent! You are perfectly perfect! You are loved completely and absolutely. There is nothing you can do to change that!

Take heart, and keep going, one small step at a time. Be patient. Look inside yourself, and learn to love what is there.

Learn to love yourself with your whole heart. Learn to gently 'cradle yourself in your own two arms' and give yourself healing. You are so much more precious than you think!

Do you think that I would forsake you *now*?
Do you really think that I would forsake you
when you need Me most?
My dear child, this is the time when I want
you to really lean on Me.
Lean right into Me, that I might bear the
weight of what you are going through.
I love you so! I love you *so*!
I *am* hearing you when you cry to Me.
Please rest in Me and let 'My heart cradle
you'. I *will* give you peace, it is My promise
to you.

Hello My child,

I write to celebrate you today.

You are safe in My heart, I love you so. I delight to see you love, and laugh, and skip with joy, so seek out the things that make you do that.

Live, and love, and dance in Me, and stay away from all that causes you suffering. Abide in Me, and I will show you the delights of My heaven. For they are all yours, and you deserve to receive every one of them.

My beloved child,
Be of good cheer!
Wake up and remember who you are.
You are a child of heaven, a child that I
delight in.
You may have travail for a while, but you
are forever safe in Me. For I am the Truth of
Divine Love. In essence, it is what you are
too.
Let go of everything else, and rest in this. It
will set you free, and once free, you will
know My joy, and you will understand all
things.
You will light up the earth with your Spirit,
for you will have found your True home in
Me.

My dear child,
My love is the Divine Love within which
all things are born. It is the Divine Love
that encompasses everything.
There is not anything that can separate
you from My love. Not war, nor famine,
nor strife, not anything! My child, you
have to understand, that My love
includes *you*, My love encompasses *you*.
Whatever situation you may find
yourself in, My love is there also. It is
impossible for it to be otherwise.
Everything created comes from within
My love. You cannot escape it.
This is eternal Truth!

Do you really think that you are worth so little? Do you really think that you are worth nothing to Me, that I would not care if you were alive, or dead?

My dearest child, you are worth *everything* to Me! I know you are suffering, and I see your travail. I know how deeply you are hurting. I know how alone you feel.

Please try and gently hold your suffering for a while though. Please try to resist the temptation to harm yourself.

No matter what your thoughts are telling you, you truly do deserve to live. You truly do deserve to be free.

Focus only on My love, *only* on My love, and you will be set free from this.

My love will redeem you.

My love will heal you.

This is My promise to you.

My dear child,
Why do you behave as though you are a
slave, when you are a free person?
Why do you hold on to your false beliefs;
beliefs that cause you suffering, and are like
a manacle around your ankle?
Look to Me. Look only to Me, and you will
begin to see, that I am the totality of love. I
am nothing else.
I am not jealousy, nor wrath, nor punishment,
nor abuse. I will not do to you what has
already been done. I am the opposite of that. I
will undo all of that. I will completely liberate
you from all of that, and you will see what a
celebration you are, and how free you are. If
you will only look to Me.

All that you fear about yourself in life,
will turn out to be untrue.
One day, you will see, that it is just the
lies, secrets, and misunderstandings of
other people – the misperceptions of
worldly living.
Love is none of these.
We come from love.
We are born into love.
We grow in love,
and we return to love.
You are love, and only that.
This is the Truth – remember it!

Hello again my precious child,
I am wondering how you are?
I am wondering what lies heavy in
your heart today?
Tell me please, that I may take it from
you, and replace it with My joy.
Let Me show you My great love for you.
Let Me show you for sure, just how much
you mean to Me.
Let Me comfort you, and lift you up.
Believe Me when I say, that you are
My treasure, and I delight in you.

I sing to you every day of My love.
I quietly sing to you of your freedom in
Me.
Like the scent of lotus flowers, My words
softly embrace you, and your heart gently
vibrates to My tune.
Oh, how I long for you to hear My song,
My heart yearns for it.
Oh, how I long for you to sing as I do,
that your perfume may be just as sweet.

My dear child,
Look within, until you find Me there.
Finding Me there, will wipe the veil from
your eyes, and show you your True Face.
I will reveal you in your essence, and then
you will truly see yourself.
True to My original design, and named
with an eternal name, you will know
yourself utterly and totally, and you will
see just what a part of heavenly love you
are. And you will know with certainty,
that you are *only* that!

Relate to yourself kindly.
Have compassion for yourself, especially
when you are being self-critical.
It is your kindness to yourself, and your
self-care that will keep you safe.
Understand that you are not the problem.
You are loved exactly as you are.
Put your hands over your heart and say:
"I am aware of my suffering.
I am not alone in feeling this.
I am wonderfully o.k.
I am beautiful just as I am.
I completely accept myself, with no
complaints about any aspect of who I am.
I choose to remember the love that I am."

Perhaps today, perhaps tomorrow, you will see your own True Self.
When you are ready, you will glimpse it, like a glint of gold inside yourself.
Then you will know, that the Truth teachings of others, are like rose petals at your feet, a path for you to walk on.
And the Truth that is you, will be the only destination, and that destination, will be your greatest freedom.

17.

It is never personal to you, when
someone is unpleasant to you. It is
usually personal to them!
Do not get snagged by them 'acting
out' onto you, putting onto you, that
which belongs somewhere else.
Just let them be!
It is nothing to fear!
It is always a call for love, and you
are the love that is needed!
You are a Divine child, called to love,
even in the most difficult of
circumstances, even when the behaviour
of others is very uncomfortable to be
around.
Keep your peace, and remember to love.

When you seek Me, you will be taken
out from amongst the false truth, that
causes you pain.
You will be taken inwards, to the altar
of your own inner Truth, where all that
is holy abides.
And you will know your True Self, and
you will know Divine Love, for they are
One.
And when you know who you truly are,
you will be overjoyed!

To be at peace,
to be in love with life,
we have to accept our oneness
with each other.
We have to accept,
that there is no separation
between us.
We are all together
on this 'path'.
It is One 'journey'.

All the leaves on all the trees, cannot stay.
The yellow sun up in the sky, cannot stay.
Your mother and your father, your brothers
and your sisters, cannot stay.
As it comes, so it will go, nothing stays.
The waves keep landing on the shore, they
touch the sand, then are no more.
Not one stays.
All the names for earthly things, get in the
way. To really know Me, they cannot stay.
Let all the leaves fall, and then you will see
Me – Hooray! Hooray!

You see, you do not believe that you can really trust Me. You think that I will let you down, that I will forget you, overlook you, or just not be bothered about you, that I will go away and leave you to suffer.

That is not true. It would be impossible for Me to do that! It is impossible, because I Am! I am everything, in everything, and of everything. It is all Me! You are of Me! I am totally in you!

It is only by the thoughts of your own mind, that you can imagine separation from Me. Let go of those thoughts. Sit silently in the space that is left by their absence, and you will find both Me and your Self there as One.

I will perform miracles for you! I will 'move mountains' for you! And when you have let go of your thought-self, and dwell in the Spirit of what I am, you will do likewise.

A flower does not choose how to bloom, it just blooms!
Be exactly who you are.
Be your own True Self.
Be the magnificence of your whole being.
Just bloom!
Just give your beauty, and your fragrance, everywhere you go.
Be exactly what you were created to be.
Show your True Face, and allow the world to see just how wonderful you are.
When the world sees *you*, it will embrace you wholeheartedly.

My dear child,
What can I say to you about self-worth?
Well, you need to have it! You need to own it!
It is yours!
Do not allow anyone to rob you of it.
You are worth so much to Me. Your value is
beyond price. You are My child, full of grace,
and light, and love.
You are a celebration of life.
You are precious.
Remember who you are!
Remember to love yourself.
Love your holy Truth, and shine your life out
into the world.
Believe in yourself.
Embrace yourself.
And fully be yourself, for you are truly
magnificent!

Wherever you are, bring your whole
awareness into the here and now, and
breathe.
Be here, now, in this moment, for it is in
this very moment, that you will be most
fully alive.
When your mind wanders, bring it back to
your breath and this present moment.
Bring yourself back, to where you are now.
Breathe in, and look around you.
Ground yourself, in where you are.
Recognise, that you are here now, in this
place.
Breathe out, and let all of your cares go out
on your breath.
Look at your surroundings, smell the air,
feel the ground beneath your feet.
Do this often, and you will find peace.

Arise! Arise! You have been 'asleep' for too long! My child, you are 'rotting'! Wake up! Wake up!

All is not as it seems. What you think is real, is just the kaleidoscope of your own perceptions, being played out, onto the dreamy 'screen' of life.

Wake up, and wipe the 'mist of sleep' from your eyes. Arise from your bed of mindlessness, and begin your journey into being wide awake.

Seek the One reality that is eternal and unchanging. For once you have found it, you will never 'fall asleep' again, and you will see all things anew, and you will see all things wonderfully!

Keep going! Do not give up!
Never give up on yourself, not even when the pain of your own suffering seems unbearable. You are definitely worth the effort. Put your hands over your heart, and tell yourself that. Your life is so precious.
You are needed.
The essence that is you, is needed.
You are so worth recovering.
If only you will keep going, there will come a time, when you will see, just how worthwhile you are, and what an incredible journey your life is, and how worth it, the pain will have been. There will come a time, when you will be able to 'move mountains', but for now, you just need to believe in yourself and keep going.

My dear child,
You see yourself as being somehow
wounded, scarred, and 'broken', and less
beautiful, and worthy, because of that, but
I do not see you in that way at all.
To Me, there is no question that you are
beautiful, and worthy. Your wounded-ness,
is gloriously beautiful to Me. It is how you
will grow in love, and compassion, and how
you will learn, what to truly value in
yourself and others.
Your wounded-ness will teach you to love
and celebrate yourself, as I love you and
celebrate you. That is – totally, absolutely
and unconditionally.

My dear child,

You can call Me by any of your names for Me, and I will answer you. My love is total, complete, and absolute. It embraces all.

I am always here for you. I am here for all. I will not hurt you, or harm you. I will never judge you, or punish you. I will not ignore you, or push you away, and I will always respect you. I will definitely embrace you. I will heal all of your worldly hurts. And you do not have to find Me, for I am already here.

When you meet Me, really meet Me, you will know Me, and you will know that I am One. And then, you will not be able to name Me at all.

You are this celebration of life, this seed
of creation, this spark of Divinity.
My dear child, you are this, when with
friends, or lovers, or parents, or workmates.
You are this, whether with teachers, or
authorities, or priests, or laymen, or people
standing on street corners.
You are this cosmic life energy.
Whether in prison or free, in weakness or
in strength, when there is love and respect,
or when there is not – you are still this.

My child, let Me sing you a lullaby.
It goes like this:
"Little Salt Doll,
sitting in a tub,
floating on the Ocean,
of Divine Love.
Living her life,
bobbing about,
longing to swim,
but scared to jump out.
She'll stay in the bathtub,
'til one day she'll begin,
to recognise clearly,
the Ocean within.
Then out of the bath,
and into the Sea,
off she will go,
totally free."
Ha, ha, ha! I love that song!

Love is the prayer of the Divine.
Love is the Messiah.
Love is God.
Love is Allah, Brahman, the Buddha—
whatever holy name you give it.
It has a thousand names, and more.
Love envelops the whole universe within
Itself.
It is the song of the fragrant heart.
It is where we dwell, and what we are
derived from.
It is the only thing that we have to give,
and the only thing that we have to
receive.
It is what we are.

My dear child,

I know that your suffering causes you great pain. And I am asking a lot, when I ask you to sit with it, and let it stay for a while, that you might get to know it better, as you would get to know a dear friend.

But if you can bear to allow that, over time, you will begin to see, that your suffering is like a mud pond, in which the most beautiful lily grows.

The 'mud' of your suffering, is the soil from which your True Self will emerge. It is the soil in which your love, tenderness, and compassion, for the whole of life, will grow.

When the 'mud' of suffering, meets the Spirit of the True Self, the 'scent of heaven' fills the air, and the suffering of all is eased.

When you sit in silence, I will sit with you. When you talk, I will listen. When you tell your story, I will not disapprove. When you share your suffering, I will weep with you. When you call out in pain, I will give you succour. When you hold out your hand in the dark, I will take hold of it. When you cannot move, for fear, I will hold you safely.

When you seek My love, I will cover you with My compassion. When you yearn for Truth, I will share it with you. When you seek acceptance, I will embrace you. When you need a blessing, I will give it as a gift.

You called? You called to Me?
I have heard you. Come! Come hither My
child, and rest in Me. For I am yours, and
you are mine, imperishable, eternally.
Escape Me? Forget you?
How could that be? I am in you, and you
are in Me. We are One, and we are Trinity
– holy, holy, holy. It is all the same!
Where have you been?
You have been here with Me. When you
have travelled, and gone away, you were in
Me. Because I am silent, you thought I
was not there. That cannot be.
Return? Return to Me?
You are still here! When will you learn? It
is safe to wander, you wander in Me! You
had forgotten, that is all, and now you will
remember!

My child,
I hear you, when you say, that you
cannot go on without love. I can feel
your loneliness in My own heart, and it
aches. I can see, that your heart wants
love, and only love, and that it will do
without everything else, if it can have just
that one thing.
And I say to you, turn to Me, for I am the
Love that you are looking for. I am that
eternal, unchanging, undying Love, that
cannot be diminished, or destroyed, and
which embraces all.
I am the Love that is everywhere, both
within, and without. I am the unavoidable
Love!
So open your heart, and you will find
Me there, and when you do, you will find
Me everywhere else also. And when you
find Me, in everything, you will be in
heaven, and you will never have to search
for love again.

My child,
In silence and in stillness, I am here.
I hear your cry to Me. I see your pain. I am
here! I see how unbearable it sometimes feels
for you. I am here!
When you breathe in, I am here.
When you breathe out, I am here.
In the still small space between each breath,
I am here.
So shout your pain and anger out at Me.
Shout it in My face. Do not hold on to any
of it. Shout it at Me until it is done with.
And then sit with Me for a while.
Sit here with Me, in the silence and the
stillness. Let your tears flow. Hold
yourself tenderly. Allow us to sit together
in this place, this place of love and healing.

My dearest child,

I have seen you sitting on the carpark roof, with your legs hanging over the edge. I have seen the scars on your wrists, from where you have harmed yourself.

I long to come and sit with you, to be by your side, and have you rest your pain weary head on My chest. For I would sing to you of My love for you, and I would give you comfort. Life can be so cruel, but love is not.

Life can batter us about, and spin us around, but love will not do that. Love is the opposite of that.

If I could sit with you, and hold you close to Me, you would feel what love is, you would know what love is, and you would know that love heals all things, and it never harms, not even oneself.

38.

You do not have to be perfect and faultless,
My child. It is not by being perfect, that
people will love you, and want you. Over
time, you will begin to realise, that it is the
exact opposite of that.
You will see, that My idea of perfection, is
very different to yours.
You will see, that people will love you, and
want you more than ever, once they have
seen your wounds, and know that you are
sometimes vulnerable, and that you sometimes make mistakes.
Because, in seeing those things in you,
they will know, that you are the same as
them, you are just like them.
And it is those things in you, that make
you perfectly perfect to Me.

My dear child,

You sit before Me, reading My little paper words, because you seek Me, and do not fully realise, that you have already found Me.

You, yes *you*, are the essence of My love. You are both the seeker and that which is sought. You are the named, and that which is beyond all names.

You are the 'lotus flower' of heaven, and also the 'soil of the earth', in which it grows.

When you experience this, and know it to be true, you will know with absolute certainty, that you and I are One – there is only One, and that One is the totality of all!

Come child, and sit here with Me for a while. Pause, stop, breathe, if only for a minute. Let go of all that busies you, and sit with Me.

We will not speak. We will just sit, and take this time together, making space, for stillness, and the peace that silence brings.

Let go of your thoughts, as best you can, and simply breathe. Allow this moment for yourself, alone and together with Me. Let your cares drift on the wind, and simply breathe. Remember who you are, at the centre of your being, and breathe. Just breathe.

My dear child,

You were born into the world, with your earthly body of flesh and bone. You live in the world of giving and receiving, gaining and losing, and you suffer your suffering. And I sigh when I see it!

For I am here, waiting, but you do not see Me. You stress and strain, and play with your own kind of happiness, and I have to just watch you 'fall'.

You fall into Me!

If only you could see that, you would melt into My arms, in a rapture of relief and joy. In Me, you would know your Self for the first time, you would know what real happiness is, and you would be reborn into heaven.

My child,

Sometimes, you will meet people that you need to just not be around. Sometimes, there will be people, who do not treat you well.

You will know in your heart, when you are not being properly loved, and respected.

When you meet such people, move away from them, as quickly as you can. Even if you are tempted to stay, do not hang around.

And then, there will be times, when you meet people, who you connect with instantly, because you can tell, that they will be good for you.

You know, that they will treat you well, and celebrate you for who you are.

Seek them out, and stay close to them, for they will nourish your Spirit, and allow its light to shine.

Peace, peace, peace! My peace I give to you.
Take it now, and hold it in your heart,
that you might rest from your burden of
toil and stress. Take a breath for yourself,
and receive My peace.

Do you think, I have not noticed the strain
you are under? Do you think, I cannot see
the fear in your eyes, and the signs of
stress upon your face?

Dear child, you have not gone un-noticed
by Me. I have come, to give My peace to
you. It is a gift. Please allow yourself to
receive it. Stop, pause, breathe, and rest in
Me.

To My little 'Eagle Child':
'Your radiant Spirit
of golden wind –
its wings are clipped,
its ankles ringed,
is sorrow stained,
and anger tinged,
but none-the-less surviving.
One day will fly,
to glorious heights,
gliding the sky
on rays of Light.
You will know in full
this boundless realm –
no – thing, but One abiding.'

My dear child,
Wherever you go in the world, I will be
behind you. Whatever you do, I will support
you. Whatever you need, I will give it to you.
If you owe money, I will pay it. If you get
lost, I will go to the ends of the earth to find
you. If you need defending, I will stand by
you. If you are wounded, I will hold you. If
you are defeated, I will lift you up.
If you spite Me, I will turn My face to one side.
If you wound Me, I will still embrace you. If
you turn away from Me, I will be waiting, for
when you come back.
You are My most beloved child, and I will
always be here for you.
Go on your way, knowing these things, and
live your life fully, as a celebration of the
beautiful Self that you are.
My love goes with you.

My child, come to Me.
Come and sit with Me. For I can see that you are deeply distressed, and needing comfort.
Come into My arms, and let Me hold you. Cling to Me, so that I can hold you close, and let you feel My warmth and love.
When your pain is unbearable, and you feel that there is nowhere to go with it, come here to Me. I am your place of safety, and I will sing to you of My love.
I will sing to you, of a love that will never leave you desolate, or comfortless. I will sing to you, of a love that will always hold you.
Even in your deepest despair, when you feel unable to look to Me, I will still hold you in My arms, and rock you gently, and sing to you of My love.

My dearest, most beloved child,
How tenderly I wish to speak with you now,
when you are faced with death, and do not
understand it well.
My child, there is nothing to fear!
Death, is when I 'scoop you up into My arms',
and carry you to the 'House of all Healing',
which is My home.
Before you were born, I carried you in Me.
Whilst you have been living on earth, I have
been carrying you in Me. After your death,
I will carry you in Me.
Moving in and out of form, you are always
in Me. Nothing is ever lost. Everything is
eternal. All is One! All is One!

Nothing ever ends, or is lost. Everything
is eternal. Things just are, shifting, and
changing, moving in and out of form.
Things are not as they first seem. Reality
is a subjective thing – a never ending
kaleidoscope of energy, dancing in the
light and dark of life.
All is One, coming together, and moving
apart. Building up, and breaking down.
Birthing, dying, rebirthing....
You are a flicker of life, dancing, dancing,
then dying into the One, only to be reborn,
into another form.

When you see My True Face, and you see that it is shining upon you constantly, and in seeing Me, you know Me for the first time, you will fall into My arms in ecstasy.

When you see, the bliss that I am, eternally, and you experience Me for the first time, you will fall into My arms in ecstasy.

When you receive My love, and you feel its touch, its warmth, its embrace, for the first time, you will fall into My arms in ecstasy.

When you see Me, for the first time, and in an inexpressible way, you know Me totally, you will fall into My arms in ecstasy.

And you will know that we are One, you and I, and you will weep with joy!

ABOUT THE AUTHOR

You do not really need to know who I am. I could be you! I could have had your life, with your joys, and your suffering, and I could have written the 'silent songs', that are already singing in your own heart. There is no big difference between us!

I am a person, who has lived a little, and experienced a lot. I have worked in child care, nursing, alternative medicine, and counselling. I have had great fun, great love, and lots of laughter, and I have also experienced abuse, ill-health, disability, and now, at 62yrs old, I am older than I used to be.

The overwhelming realisation about my life, is that for me, love is the most important thing. Love is everything. I am learning to surrender myself to it, to love myself, and to love all others. This is a life-long journey, and I am still only quite near the beginning!

Neti.

©Neti has asserted her right under the Copyright,
Designs and Patent Act 1988 to
be identified as the author of this book.

This book has been published
by Kindle Direct Publishing.

©All rights are reserved.
This publication may not be copied, stored,
or transmitted, without written consent
from the author.

ISBN: 9781723774782

Printed in Poland
by Amazon Fulfillment
Poland Sp. z o.o., Wrocław

54145039R00069